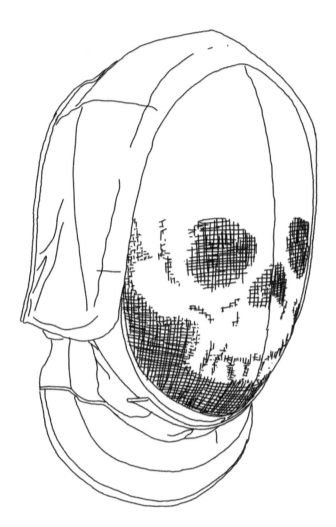

THE HELM OF CAPTAIN MABERU

This book is dedicated to:

My wife, Cherelyn, who has to deal with all of my shenanigans and loves me anyway.

My son, Christian, who shared many mornings with me going to keiko.

My friend, Tyler, who started this crazy path with me.

DISCLAIMER:

This book is for informational and entertainment purposes only. The information in this book is only meant as a supplement for what you are learning at your martial arts school or saber group and is not meant to replace your instructor's training. You should discuss and review multiple techniques and exercises with your instructor.

Martial arts can be dangerous. People can and do get hurt, even when properly trained. You should only train and practice under the supervision of a skilled instructor and with the proper equipment. All children practicing these skills should be supervised by a trained instructor and their parents. Parents should discuss with their child's instructor what is and what is not appropriate training for their child.

Martial arts training and physical conditioning can be very physically demanding. Make sure that you check with a doctor before starting any intense exercise regime in order to avoid injuries and aggravating any potential medical condition (i.e. heart problem). If you get hurt, please see a doctor! This book does not provide any medical advice.

Readers of this book cannot use and shall not allow any person to use the information in this book in any way that violates a federal, state, or local law, regulation, or ordinance, or for any illegal purpose,

By practicing any of the techniques listed or shown in this book, you are assuming full responsibility for your own actions and any injury that may result from your actions. The information in this book is only intended for martial arts training and not for any illegal or violent behavior.

Please enjoy responsibly.

Table of Contents

Preface..……............ i

Introduction...……........ ii-vii

1) Building on Solid Ground: Two-Handed
   Techniques...1-51

2) Building strength, Speed, and Awareness: One-Handed
   Techniques.. 53-71

3) The Art of the Duel: Technique in
   Action................................…..…...73-95

THE WAY OF THE WARPRIDER

A Beginner's Guide to Practical Lightblade Dueling.
By: David James Willet

01/05/2021
PREFACE

We've all heard the stories: long ago, and in a galaxy far, far away the Jedi were the keepers of peace and justice for over a thousand generations. During that time their prowess with a laser-sword was unparalleled. They trained to use this weapon from the time they were small children and many perfected their skills over time with the help of a teacher.

However, for us here in the mundane world of everyday reality, most blade practitioners don't begin to develop our skills until we are much older. Without a formal teacher, we must stand on the shoulders of giants to peer into this world and grasp at the unknown. We are seeking a purpose that we find in the glowing blade.

We use that knowledge to propel our bodies forward with determination. Information from many classical and modern sources can be put together to form a cohesive method with which to wage mock war against our friends and fellow seekers who feel compelled to pick up a blade and enter the field of combat.

This is the way of the Warprider.

INTRODUCTION

This book does not claim to represent the totality of all of the possible stances, styles, or techniques that exist for the art of the Light-bladed weapons. I do not adhere to any one style, but instead seek out techniques that will help to turn the tide of battle in my favor through real-time dueling.

The information that I have compiled here represent some of the techniques that I would regularly use in a duel on any given day and they have served me well. You must practice these principles repeatedly in order to master them. The information contained in this book is the totality of all of the information that my lightsaber group, The Central Republic (also called TCR), would go over with new members. The focus is to help new fighters build a strong foundation with which to move forward. I have also included information that many beginners struggle with, or simply wouldn't know unless someone focused on it specifically. When possible, I shall try and use generic terms when describing movements or actions, so they are applicable to either right or left-handed fighters; otherwise, my default will be right-handed.

My goal with this book is to prepare fighters of all ages for their first duel. You may already have a saber or you may be using a broom handle or PVC pipe for your solo practice; it doesn't matter. These techniques will help you develop your proficiency with a blade either way. If you haven't gotten a blade yet and want some cursory information about selecting your first weapon, please read on... the next section details some basic information about sabers in general without showing a preference to a specific brand or type. Each lightsaber hilt has several parts:

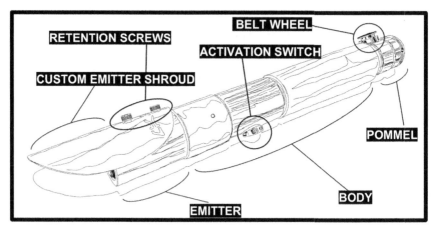

Not pictured: the charging port. Most sabers are rechargeable these days and many come with a "kill-key," which is a small plug that inserts into the charging port to disable the saber when not in use and prevent battery drain or unintended ignition of the saber. The charging port may be located near the Activation switch or elsewhere on the chassis itself.

Make sure you do your research before you decide to purchase your first saber.

Sabers vary greatly in quality and pricing, so it's important to become familiar with these weapons, the differences between them, and which blades will work best for the rigor that a serious duel requires. If you are serious about dueling, it would be better to avoid the mass-produced toy sabers and search online lightsaber vendors because they tend to be more durable and have more options and customization opportunities.

However, be aware that not all saber retailers sell proprietary goods. Many retailers are essentially just retailers who are licensed to sell sabers manufactured by other vendors at a slight markup. It pays to do your research. Generally speaking, I use what is known as a "base-lit" saber with an ultra-heavy blade:

Base-lit
This means that the lightsaber functions essentially like a flashlight; it's an aluminum handle with a switch and a light in the emitter. The difference is that these will also have a polycarbonate blade and could have an electronics package for sound and/or color changing, flash-on-clash or other sound effects. There are many resources available online that will help you find the right one for you. Sabers can be purchased with an LED strip in the blade as well, and many of the manufacturers and customizers swear that they are durable, but I'm not sure that they will survive heavy dueling as well as a base-lit saber.

Blades
Light saber blades are essentially polycarbonate tubes (plastic) that have a length of rolled up plastic vellum inside to make the blade appear more solid (sorry if I just ruined the magic for

you). There is an acrylic cap called a "blade tip" on the end of the blade to keep everything inside and help maintain the lightsaber appearance. These tips can be pointed or rounded depending on your preference. Keep in mind that many saber groups don't allow pointed blade-tips due to the possibility of injury from their use.

The blades come in different lengths and thicknesses, but are generally either clear or white. You can get a colored plastic blade known as a dayblade that is intended to be used during the day. A thin-walled blade is much lighter and thus more maneuverable and quicker than a thick (or ultra-heavy) blade, but it is much weaker. The thicker plastic blade is quite strong and is intended for heavy dueling.

Interior Electronics

The electronics can vary greatly by manufacturer, and often, much of the expense involved with buying a saber comes from whatever card comes with the saber. Saber electronics can range from "stunt" sabers which have in-hilt LED to high-end display pieces that have a complex chassis holding the soundboard and connected to a string of LEDs inside the blade. Many of the high-end sabers do advertise that they are duel-ready, but the safe bet is to get something durable and functional so that if and when you damage your saber, you don't have to worry about the cost so much.

During my time dueling I have acquired five sabers from different manufacturers; three of them have broken while dueling. Luckily most of the issues revolved around the wiring or plastic components and not the light and sound card itself, so anyone with basic electrical knowledge can perform the repairs themselves.

Hilt design

is an important aspect of choosing your saber that people often overlook. You might like the idea of assuming a Sith-type character with sharp pokey things on the saber hilt, but most, if not all dueling organizations prohibit spikes, blades, or dangerous projections on your saber because they may cause very real injury to your opponent or their equipment. Also, some sabers have narrow sections which act as effective pivot points and allow better movement while dueling one-handed. Cross-bar sabers have smaller blade projections that jut out of the top of the emitter and provide some extra combat potential if used correctly. You can also purchase staffs (double-bladed sabers) and pikes (single-bladed, long-handled sabers), and each one has their advantages and disadvantages.

A Saber-staff (below) can be a formidable weapon in the right hands, but you must remember that it's physically two sabers that are joined at the pommel. You do get the bonus of having a second blade to strike with, and an extended reach on some strikes, but it does have a disadvantage of being twice as heavy as a single saber and the second blade can actually be a huge disadvantage until you become proficient with the weapon.

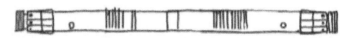

Classic Double-Bladed Saber-staff

A lightsaber pike is essentially a Saber-staff with one of the blades removed. It is heavier than a single-bladed saber, but is made a little easier to handle without the second blade of the Saber-staff. Plus, with the longer handle, you get the bonus extension through your reach and can execute strikes that are outside of your opponent's strike zone. A creative duelist constantly looks for opportunities to create a more efficient strike. Make sure you consider everything when shopping for a new saber.

The cross-guard saber (above) is similar to the two-handed broadswords that were used by knights in ancient Europe. Techniques that emphasize power and direct lines of attack would be ideal for sabers of this type. The cross-guard blades can be helpful because they would stop your opponent's blade from sliding down and striking your hands or wrists. They can also be an additional attack device if you get close enough with them to make contact with your opponent. Unfortunately, they can also be a hidden danger to the user because you must be careful not to strike yourself with the crossbar as well.

The curved hilt of the saber above also has its advantages in combat. This saber is meant for one-handed specialization and techniques. Wielders of this saber should be very skilled as the curve provides greater finesse and precision in a duel. Lunges, strikes, and parries consistent with modern European fencing techniques should be considered while using a curved hilt.

This shoto saber (above) would work well for one-handed combat, or as an off-hand sword while dual-wielding. The style used with this sword would be more in line with Japanese short-sword (wakizashi) fighting, such as the famous "Two-Skies" method. The blade on a shoto is typically shorter than a full-sized two-handed saber for ease of maneuverability and quick movements. They work well in close-quarter dueling since they require less room to navigate, but they aren't as effective as the solo weapon in a duel because of the shorter length of the hilt and the blade which rob you of their reach.

Lightsaber Hangers

Lightsabers can be worn with the blade removed if you insert a blade-plug into the emitter to prevent damage to the LED unit. There are two main types, but creativity is king so fighters are constantly coming up with new ways to brandish their saber. Here are a few of the most common:

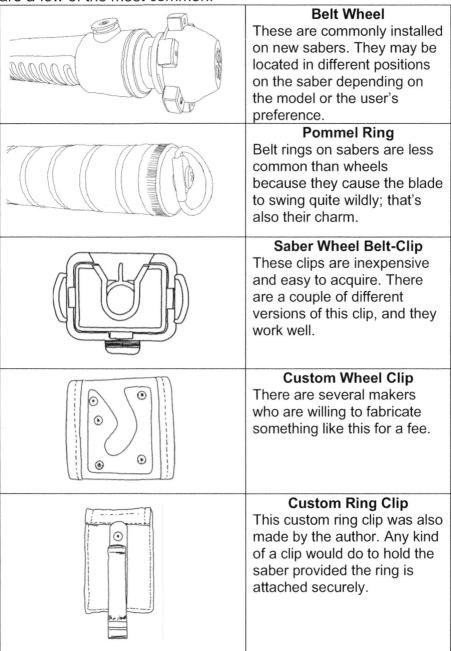

	Belt Wheel These are commonly installed on new sabers. They may be located in different positions on the saber depending on the model or the user's preference.
	Pommel Ring Belt rings on sabers are less common than wheels because they cause the blade to swing quite wildly; that's also their charm.
	Saber Wheel Belt-Clip These clips are inexpensive and easy to acquire. There are a couple of different versions of this clip, and they work well.
	Custom Wheel Clip There are several makers who are willing to fabricate something like this for a fee.
	Custom Ring Clip This custom ring clip was also made by the author. Any kind of a clip would do to hold the saber provided the ring is attached securely.

1) Building on solid ground: Two-Handed Techniques

As you begin your journey to become proficient with a Laser-sword, I would begin where most younglings begin; with the two-handed saber techniques.

Basic Ready-stances and proper grip.

Let's start with your **grip**. It's important to grip the sword correctly for proper movement when striking, blocking and parrying.

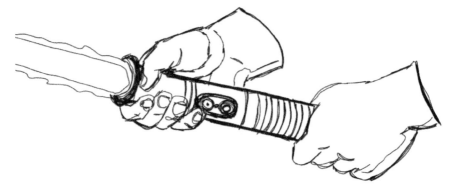

Demonstration of proper two-handed grip.

If you are a traditional right-handed sword wielder, your top hand will be your right hand. Your bottom hand will be your left hand and your hands should be about one hand-width apart. Your top hand offers directional control to your saber and should be loose and agile. Resist the urge to choke or squeeze the end of the lightsaber. Your bottom hand adds power to the swing and provides stability to your lightsaber. You should keep a firm grip on the bottom of your saber to provide strong control along your body's center line. Don't hold your saber with a death-grip. Both hands should allow your saber to move freely and change direction when needed. Too firm of a grip will slow you down!

DO NOT GRIP THE LIGHTSABER LIKE A BASEBALL BAT OR AN AXE!

Next is the basic "**Ready-stance**." This is also called a receiving stance or middle guard, and it's basically just a way to signal to your opponent that you are ready to fight while keeping your center line covered. The details for this stance are below.
The fighter is facing their opponent with both hands on their blade using the proper grip (as mentioned above).

The lightsaber is held out in front of the fighter with the tip of the blade pointed at their opponent's throat. If you were to rotate 360° you would create your "Circle of Death." Prepare to attack and destroy anything enters your circle. Your shoulders should be relaxed and loose. Don't lean too far forward like a lot of fighters tend to do. Instead, balance your weight evenly

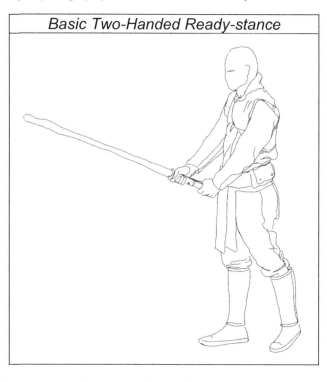

Basic Two-Handed Ready-stance

between your feet and keep your back straight. The blade should be held about a fist's width away from your belly, at or slightly below the navel—that is your center, and is the source of your energy.

Don't lock your elbows. The arms should be strong and fluid. If you lock your joints; shoulders, knees, elbows, etc., you will slow your strikes and you'll feel your body resist your movements. The left foot is in front and is pointed at the opponent. The weight is on the ball of the foot and not the heel. The right foot should be at a 45° angle about a foot-length behind your lead foot. For this stance, don't spread your feet too far apart and keep your knees loose and ready to strike (NOT locked!)

Other stances can be used depending on your situation or your intent. The Basic Ready-Stance, also called the Middle-Guard, is a solid, straight-forward stance that protects the center body mass (a major strike point) while allowing the fighter to have easy attack or defense abilities and movement around the combat area. The important thing to remember with this stance, and with this first form in general, is that form and posture are key!

Don't let your form get lazy or weak. Always maintain proper stances and movements in order to remain effective and correctly utilize this primary dueling form. There are other guards as well; upper, middle, and lower guard positions are covered below. In your research you will undoubtedly uncover several different versions of this form, and I have covered several different types of forward guard stances on the following pages.

"Push & Pull" basic hand movements.

A good two-handed strike should involve more than just bringing the blade up and down. When bringing the saber up to wind up a strike, the top hand should pull the blade back toward you as your arms bring it back. The bottom hand should push the pommel away from you at the same time. When you bring the saber back down toward your target, your top hand will push the blade away from you. The bottom hand will pull the pommel toward your body as your arms guide both your hands and saber toward your target.

If you use the kendo style of fencing, the push and pull method can be used for any strike, but the movements are intended to be swift and direct. Maintain a rigid posture and control the plane of battle like the ancient samurai who originated these techniques!

When you use the **Push & Pull** method of saber control, you help the blade move quicker to its destination. Quicker movement equals quicker strikes and quicker defense when you need it.

Push & Pull

Winding up a strike
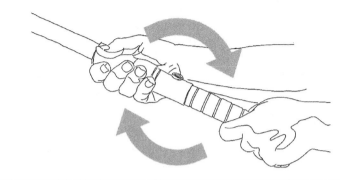
As you raise the saber up, begin the Push & Pull motion at the same time. The top hand pulls the blade back and the bottom hand pushes the pommel out. The shoulders should be relaxed, but make sure to maintain your posture. With time and practice this technique will become second nature.
Delivering a strike
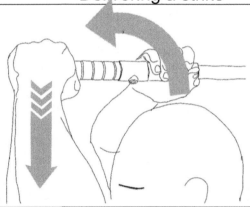
You use the reverse motion as you lower the blade downward. If you are delivering a strike, the top hand pushes the blade down and away from your body. The bottom hand pulls the blade toward your body. The upper grip should be fluid and loose, and the bottom hand should be firm, but don't squeeze the pommel.

Standard overhead strike (without footwork)

Start in ready position	
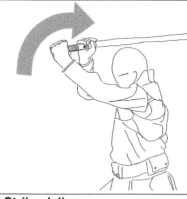	Strikes can begin from any ready position, but the standard ready-stance is being used here. The top hand is on the emitter and the bottom hand is gripping the pommel. The top hand`s job is to guide the blade along its path; in this case it guides the blade straight along the fighter's centerline to a position above the forehead. The power in the strike comes from the bottom hand, which also moves vertically along the fighter's center axis.
Prepare the strike	
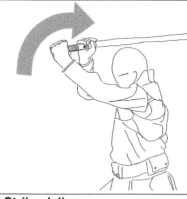	Bring the blade up above the forehead until it is just parallel to the ground. The top hand should be loose and guides the blade into position with a pulling motion. The bottom hand powers the strike along the fighter's center axis with a pushing motion. Don't stop the blade in front of your face or bend too far back. Use this "push & pull" method to move your blade around with every strike.
Strike delivery	
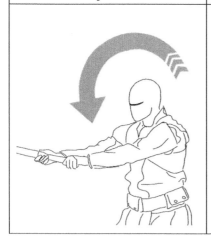	Use "push & pull" to bring the blade down toward your opponent. This time, your top hand should be pushing the blade forward and your bottom hand should be pulling the pommel inward at the same time. Your target should be the center of your enemy's forehead. Do not lean forward or drop your head during the strike. Keep your back straight and don't lock or snap your elbows as you strike. When you are done, return to ready-stance or complete your second action.

After you strike, quickly return to the ready position. Your strike may not have hit your opponent, so you need to be ready for your next move.

Attack/Guard Positions

Wide Stance/High Guard

The feet in Wide Stance are traditionally set slightly wider than shoulder width apart. The knees should be bent, but fluid. Keep the thighs tight and ready to launch. The front foot should point at your opponent and your back foot should be at a 45-degree angle. Keep your weight evenly placed between them. The front foot should be placed actually in front of your body and your back foot should be behind you. The saber should be held high, slightly above the forehead, and the elbows should be spread apart. Hold the saber at a 45-degree angle with the tip pointed at the sky behind you. Keep your back straight and position your body so that your torso and pelvis are facing your opponent.

The Wide Stance is ideal for unstable terrain, but can be used in most any situation.

The wide footing can be used to widen the stance of other guard forms.

In this version of the stance, the feet are placed about shoulder-width apart. Your arms should be in the same position as with the basic ready-stance. Take care not to lean forward while doing this stance because your body will tend to lean forward to balance yourself.

Practice balancing your weight with your back straight and get a feel for it until it becomes natural. That will help you build strength and stamina, as well as prevent you from leaning out too far and getting struck in the head

High (Inverted) Guard

Keep your feet in the standard ready position, and raise your arms above your head with the blade held at a 45° angle. Keep your elbows out and the hilt of your sword should be almost touching the top of your head.

This is a quick-strike position. You don't need to wind up and strike because the blade is already there.

This position is also a minor taunt because it appears to your opponent that you have left your leg open for a strike so they may move in closer and give you the opportunity to strike first.

Knight's Guard

This guard is one of the most iconic stances of this first form.

The feet can be in classic position or wide stance. The saber is held with the hilt next to the fighter's face and the blade held completely vertical. The body is turned mostly sideways to your opponent.

This stance allows for quick strikes, but also leaves room for other options and strikes, allows for quick walking movement around the combat area, and the fighter can switch between right and left side quickly.

Low Forward Guard

This guard requires a strong lower body and back.

The feet are wide and planted firmly. The back is straight and the head is defiantly pointed at your opponent.

The blade is held in front with the blade pointed deceptively at your opponent's feet. The arms and legs are taught and ready to strike first!

This stance could take some practice to master because it leaves much of your body exposed and vulnerable to attack.

This stance is a major taunt to your opponent, but it is a dangerous one.

The feet are placed in the wide stance, the blade is angled away from your opponent, and the tip of the blade is pointing behind you at a 45° angle.

The fighter appears unprepared to meet an attack, but the blade is hidden behind the fighter and is ready to strike.

Basic Footwork

Proper footwork is incredibly important, but it feels clunky at first. After a bit of practice, it will become second nature to you. These step sequences are intended to use very little movement and thus very little energy while dueling. Economy of one's personal energy is very important while facing an opponent in the combat arena. When you move to avoid a strike, or move into position to launch your own attack, you should aim to use as little energy as possible so you can unleash that energy on your opponent when you strike. The first method is the **shuffle-step**, and is described in three parts.

1. Basic **forward movement.** With your body in ready stance position, slide the front foot (◄1◄◄◄) forward about a foot and then pull the back foot (◄2◄◄◄) up until you're back in ready position, then repeat. While doing the shuffle step, your feet should not be stepping; that is to say that you should be sliding the feet forward and not actually picking them up and putting them down. (*See below*)

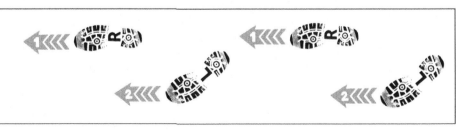

2. If you are retreating from your opponent or walking backwards, slide the back foot (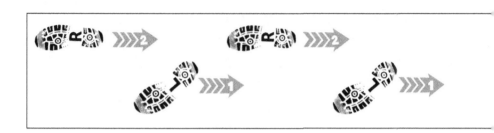) backwards a length and then bringing your front foot ( ) back to return you to your ready stance. The movement should only be in your feet and legs. Your hips, shoulders, and most importantly, your saber, should remain in your chosen stances' position. (See below)

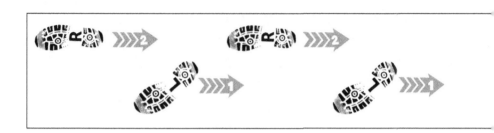

3. When using this stepping method to move sideways, the same sliding step will be used. If you are moving to the RIGHT you would begin movement with the RIGHT foot ( ), followed by the LEFT foot ( ). If you are moving to the LEFT, you begin movement with the LEFT foot, followed by the RIGHT foot in the correct direction that you are intending to travel. This is the same for right or left-handed fighters.

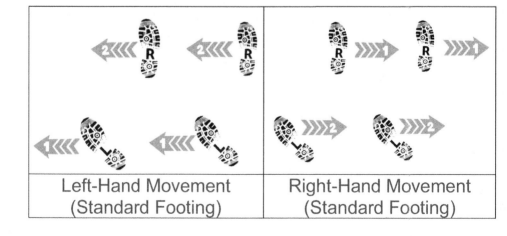

| Left-Hand Movement (Standard Footing) | Right-Hand Movement (Standard Footing) |

The next method is the **walking step**. In this method, you can pick the feet up slightly while placing one foot in front of the other while walking forward. Your body shifts position a bit as you use the walking step, but the other principles are the same: keep your shoulders relaxed, your blade pointed at your opponent's throat, and don't lock your knees.

The walking step is broken down here into four movements, for clarity, but when you perform them in practice, you should strive to complete the movements as smoothly and continuously as if you were walking. (See the next page.)

Begin in the standard Ready Position. Then step the LEFT foot forward around the RIGHT foot as if you were walking. Remember not to lift your foot too far off of the ground as you step—it's "stepping" not "stomping!"

When you get your front foot in position, slide your heel over so that you are now in what is essentially the reverse Ready Stance: your left foot should be in front and your right foot should now be in the back.

Next, step the RIGHT foot around your LEFT foot until it is back in front position. Keep your feet close to the floor and maintain your balance as you step.

Finally, rotate your LEFT heel over to put you back in the Basic Ready Position. It's important to remember to slide your heels (steps II and IV) because that will help you to maintain your balance.

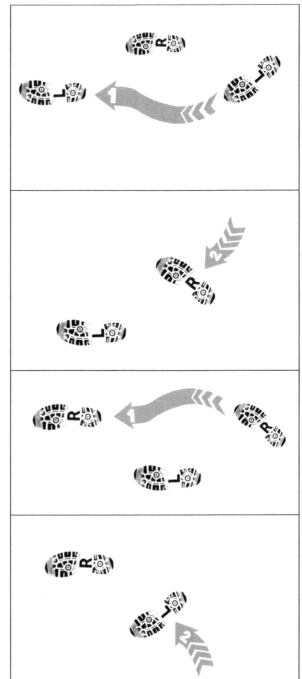

When moving sideways with the walking step, you can use the **crossing step**. Timing is important with this step, to make sure that you don't give your opponent the opportunity to cause you to trip over your own feet. (Default right-handed example) To move to the left with the crossing step, you begin by shifting your weight to your left foot and moving your right foot across and in front of you. Then, while your legs are crossed, shift your weight to your right foot and move your left foot back to your chosen ready stance. (See below)

Back foot crosses behind the right foot	Front foot crosses in front of the back foot	Return to ready stance or keep walking

It's possible to complicate this walking method even further if you continue walking to the side. The walking pattern is below:

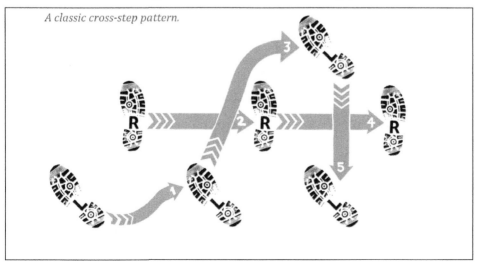

A classic cross-step pattern.

It's important to know which type of step to use for your current situation. These steps can be used in different ways depending on your duel, or the terrain, or the techniques you're using. Each step should be deliberate and your weight must be placed on the correct foot to prevent you from being off balance.

Practice each step by itself, with or without a blade in hand.

Next page:
Overhead strike with footwork.

The example for this strike will use the shuffling step with the default right-hand delivery.

1. Ready position	4. Begin strike

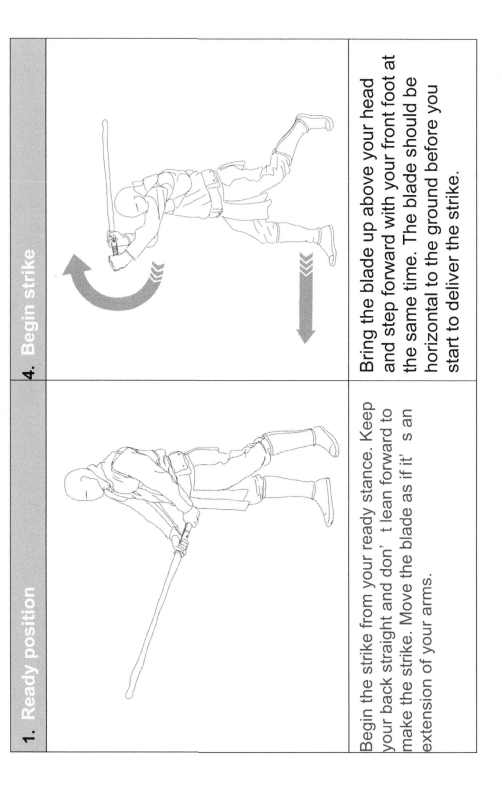

Begin the strike from your ready stance. Keep your back straight and don' t lean forward to make the strike. Move the blade as if it' s an extension of your arms.

Bring the blade up above your head and step forward with your front foot at the same time. The blade should be horizontal to the ground before you start to deliver the strike.

5. Deliver the cut	4. Reset to Ready

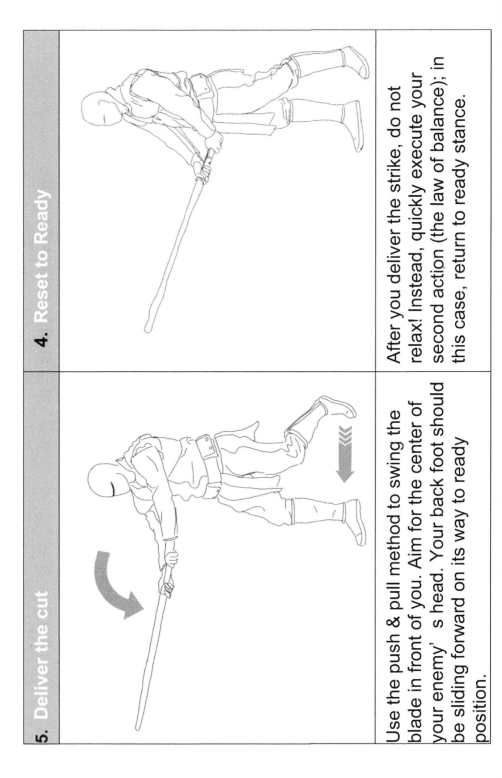

5. Deliver the cut

Use the push & pull method to swing the blade in front of you. Aim for the center of your enemy's head. Your back foot should be sliding forward on its way to ready position.

4. Reset to Ready

After you deliver the strike, do not relax! Instead, quickly execute your second action (the law of balance); in this case, return to ready stance.

The following non-examples are demonstrating some common mistakes that you should avoid while making this strike. Pay close attention to the fighter's posture and the position of the sword, etc. Read the descriptions to go with each one as well.

Extending too far back.

Timing is important in a duel. If you swing your blade back as far as you can, it will take you longer to return the swing and make a strike! Plus, pulling a strike back all of the way adds a pointless amount of momentum to your strikes which robs your accuracy and telegraphs your moves to your opponent. Excessive momentum can cause you to injure your opponent, which, as we have discussed, is a great way to alienate your friends and ensure that you'll be practicing solo!

Extending too far forward.

If you extend too far forward while delivering a strike you risk throwing yourself off balance and you will take more time to recover from the overreach leaving you vulnerable. Don't be so concerned with striking your opponent that you expose yourself to getting hit in the process.

It's important to maintain proper form while dueling so you keep the edge in combat. Once you have the edge, don't give it to your opponent by being sloppy.

Extending too far to the side.

Always do your best to maintain your posture while dueling. Reaching too far over, forgetting your footwork, or leaving a part of your body open and vulnerable to attack will get you hit by your opponent's blade.

Opportunities to strike your opponent come around again and again, don't sacrifice your part in the duel just to try and make a strike. Maintain your posture, balance and footwork as much as possible.

Two-handed Strike variations

There are many different strike types and variations; these listed here are simply some of the different strike variations that exist.

Left Side Strike	
1. Begin in Ready position	2. Wind up the strike
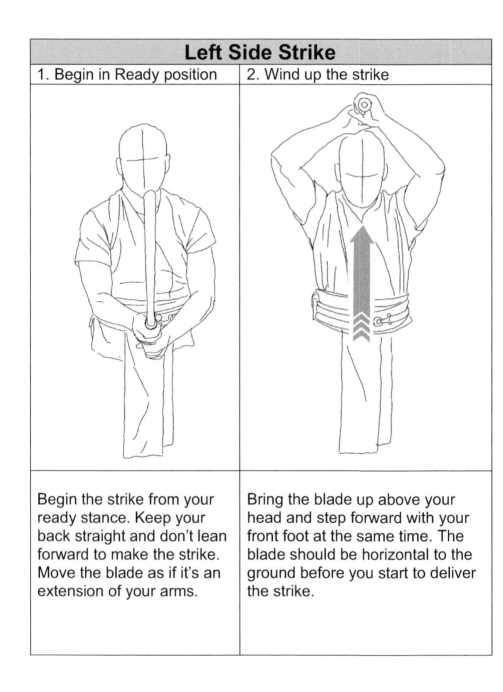	
Begin the strike from your ready stance. Keep your back straight and don't lean forward to make the strike. Move the blade as if it's an extension of your arms.	Bring the blade up above your head and step forward with your front foot at the same time. The blade should be horizontal to the ground before you start to deliver the strike.

3. Guide the blade around	4. Deliver the cut
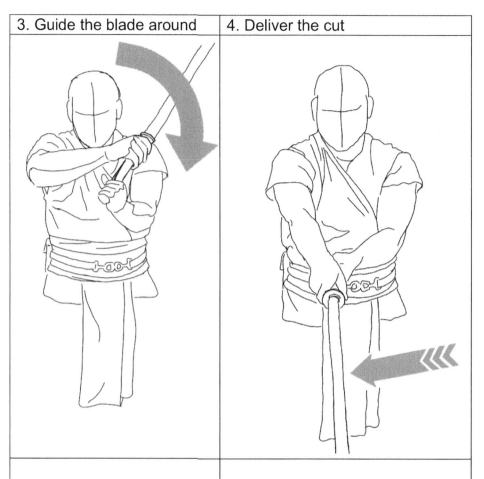	
Use the push & pull method to swing the blade over your left shoulder. Your top hand should guide the blade in a semi-circle around your left side. Your bottom hand should guide the blade along your center line up and down.	The cut should begin on your left side and end on your right. At the end, your blade should be traveling more or less horizontally. Let your arms snap the strike and then quickly move into your next action before your opponent strikes back.

Always maintain your posture as you swing. If you don't hit your target, regroup and go at it again!

Right Side Strike

1. Begin in Ready position	2. Wind up the strike

Begin the strike from your ready stance. Keep your back straight and don't lean forward to make the strike. Move the blade as if it's an extension of your arms.	Bring the blade up above your head and step forward with your front foot at the same time. The blade should be horizontal to the ground before you start to deliver the strike.

3. Guide the blade around	4. Deliver the cut

Use the push & pull method to swing the blade over your right shoulder. Your top hand should guide the blade in a semi-circle around your right side. Your bottom hand should guide the blade along your center line up and down.	The cut should begin on your right side and end on your left. At the end, your blade should be traveling more or less horizontally. Let your arms snap the strike and then quickly move into your next action before your opponent strikes back if they are able to.

Left Sweeping Strike

1. Start in Ready Position	2. Disengage

Begin the strike in the Basic Ready Stance. Your top hand guides the movement of the blade through its arc. The hand should be loose and the wrist should remain mobile and not locked. The bottom hand adds power to the strike and moves the saber along the fighter's central axis. Maintain your posture through the strike	Disengage and begin moving the blade toward your left shoulder. The path of the blade should come from the top hand. Keep your bottom hand close to your center line. Maintain your posture as you bring the blade back. The motion should come from the arms, not the body. Be certain not to pull back your blade so far that you make contact with your shoulder. Strikes to yourself count as a strike for your opponent.

3. Begin the sweep	4. Prepare for Delivery

Use the top hand to rotate the blade backwards around your left side. The top hand should be loose; just a couple of fingers will be enough to guide your blade along its path. The bottom hand provides power to the swing and keeps the saber steady. Your grip should be tight, but mobile. Don't tense up, and don't lean too much. Just guide the saber though to the next step.	Continue to guide the blade around and across your body. Your top hand should be providing the rotation arc of your saber. The hand is still somewhat loose and beginning to push the blade toward your opponent. The bottom hand should grip the pommel firmly, but don't tighten the wrist. The bottom hand still needs to follow the saber along the rotation that the top hand is guiding.

5. Deliver the Strike	6. Return to Ready Position

Bring the blade up to chest level until it is just parallel to the ground. Your actual target is around the level of your opponent's ribs or lower. The top hand should be firmly gripping the saber and guiding the blade into position with a pulling motion. The bottom hand powers the strike through along the fighter's center axis with a pushing motion to end on your right side. Use this "push & pull" method to move your blade around whenever possible.	Do not lean forward or drop your head during the strike. Keep your back straight and don't lock or snap your elbows. When you are done, return to ready-stance or complete your second action. Post-strike is also a good time to step back a bit to keep you out of your enemy's reach.

Right Sweeping Strike

1. Start in Ready Position	2. Disengage

Begin the strike in the Basic Ready Stance. Your top hand guides the movement of the blade through its arc. The hand should be loose and the wrist should remain mobile and not locked. The bottom hand adds power to the strike and moves the saber along the fighter's central axis. Maintain your posture through the strike	Disengage and begin moving the blade toward your right shoulder. The path of the blade should come from the top hand. Keep your bottom hand close to your center line. Maintain your posture as you bring the blade back. The motion should come from the arms, not the body. Be certain not to pull back your blade so far that you make contact with your shoulder. Strikes to yourself count as a strike for your opponent.

3. Begin the sweep	4. Prepare for Delivery
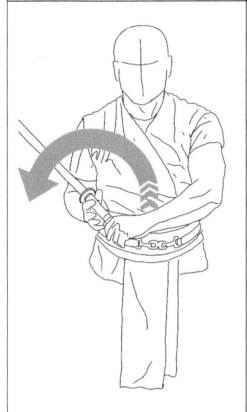	
Use the top hand to rotate the blade backwards around your right side. The top hand should be loose; just a couple of fingers will be enough to guide your blade along its path. The bottom hand provides power to the swing and keeps the saber steady. Your grip should be tight, but mobile. Don't tense up, and don't lean too much. Just guide the saber though to the next step.	Continue to guide the blade around and across your body. Your top hand should be providing the rotation arc of your saber. The hand is still somewhat loose and beginning to push the blade toward your opponent. The bottom hand should grip the pommel firmly, but don't tighten the wrist. The bottom hand still needs to follow the saber along the rotation that the top hand is guiding.

5. Deliver the Strike	6. Return to Ready Position

Bring the blade up to chest level until it is just parallel to the ground. Your actual target is around the level of your opponent's ribs or lower. The top hand should be firmly gripping the saber and guiding the blade into position with a pulling motion. The bottom hand powers the strike through along the fighter's center axis with a pushing motion to end on your left side. Use this "push & pull" method to move your blade around whenever possible.	Do not lean forward or drop your head during the strike. Keep your back straight and don't lock or snap your elbows. When you are done, return to ready-stance or complete your second action. Post-strike is also a good time to step back a bit to keep you out of your enemy's reach.

Safety First!

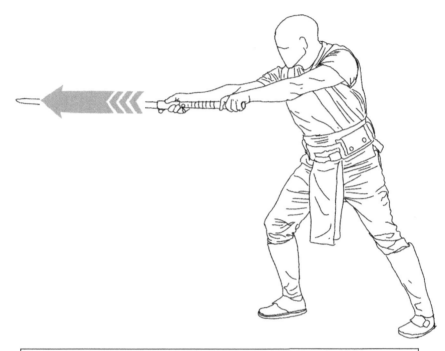

The Forbidden Strike

For safety reasons, sword strokes which use a thrusting or stabbing motion should not be used. Those moves are capable of causing real injury to an opponent, with or without protective equipment. Remember: although we seek to defeat our opponents in battle, we must be cautious not to actually harm another combatant.

BASIC BLOCKS/PARRIES

The blocks in this section are placed beside the Basic Ready Stance for a frame of reference.

There are many different types of blocks and parries that a fighter can perform during a duel, but there is an important distinction between these two words:

BLOCK

Block: to stop the movement of your enemy's sword using the blade of your own weapon. In the case of a block, the defending fighter must remain firm and they are the ones who absorb most of the force from the attack.

PARRY

Parry: to deflect the movement of your enemy's sword with your weapon. In this case the fighter's intention should be not only to block the enemies strike, but also to actually move their blade away to possibly create an opening for yourself, or knock the enemy off balance.

The parry is always superior to the block because it leaves you in the correct position to perform your second action, strike, block, or move, etc.

Right Overhead block	Left Overhead block

In this block, the foot position is basically the same as in the basic ready stance, except that the back foot should fall back a bit and your weight should shift to your back foot to pull you away from your opponent. Your arms bring the sword hilt up above your forehead and the blade should be tilted away from your head to deflect the opposing blade away from hitting your head or hands.	The left overhead block requires a change in footwork to put the fighter's body in the correct position. The front foot must slide back in a walking step and the back foot will become the front foot. The blade swings over to cover the left side of the head and shoulders. The blade must angle away to deflect blows to your head and hands. Push against your enemy's strike to parry.

Right Middle Block	Left Middle Block

The foot position is basically the same as in the basic ready stance, except that the back foot should fall back a bit and your weight must shift to your back foot to pull you away from your opponent. Bring the hilt to your waist and the blade should be tilted away from your head to deflect the opposing blade from your head or hands. Push against your enemy's strike to parry.	This block requires a change in footwork to put the fighter's body in the correct position. The front foot must slide back in a walking step and the back foot will become the front foot. The blade swings over to cover the left side. The blade must angle away to deflect blows to your left side. Push against your enemy's strike to parry.

Lower Right block	Lower Left block

This block requires a change in footwork to put the fighter's body in the correct position. The front foot must slide back in a walking step and the back foot will become the front foot. The blade swings down with the tip pointing at the floor to cover the right side, the blade must angle away from the body to deflect blows to your side and hands. Push against your attacker's blade to parry.	The foot position is basically the same as in the basic ready stance, except that the back foot should fall back and your weight should shift back to pull you away. Bring the sword hilt to chest level and the tip of the blade should be pointed at the floor. Push against your enemy's strike to parry.

COMBINATION DRILLS

Many strikes can and should be used in combination with blocks or other strikes to make a sort of "1-2" combination while dueling. Once you know the strikes and blocks you can combine them with lethal effectiveness against your opponents. On the following pages are some options for combinations that will help you be more effective in combat.

5-Strike Stepping Drill

1. Start from the Basic Ready Stance.	2. Begin Overhead Strike.
Your body should be tight, but not stiff. Don't tighten your shoulders or lock your knees. Look straight ahead and maintain your posture throughout this entire exercise.	Use the Push & Pull motion to move the blade above your head until its horizontal, and step forward with your lead foot at the same time. Don't lean back or pull the blade too far back as you prepare your strike.

3. Release your Overhead Strike.	4. Wind up your next strike (right side strike)
Again, use the push & pull motion, but this time you'll be projecting the blade in front of you. As you swing you should bring your back foot forward until your feet are about a foot apart. Your target is your enemy's forehead. Don't lock your elbows on your strike,	Bring your blade up again and prepare for your next strike. Continue walking in the shuffle-step for this strike, and throughout this exercise. Be careful not to lose your balance as your move and strike. The blade should be roughly parallel to the floor. Don't pull it back too far.

5. Release your side-strike	6. Wind up your left side strike
To complete this strike, you will begin rotating the blade around your left side. The bottom hand will provide the strength for your strike. Your top hand provides the circular movement through its path to end on your right side at about shoulder level.	Rotate the blade back towards the left side. Picture turning the tip of the blade in a big circle above your head. The top hand will again provide most of the movement. Don't pull the pommel too close into your body, but keep it held slightly in front of you for ease of movement.

7. Deliver your left side strike	8. Prepare your left-side sweep
Continue the rotation of the blade through its circuitous path. This strike will end on your left side at about shoulder level. Be careful to maintain your posture and don't lean into the strike.	Continue stepping forward and bring your blade up on your left side. This should be done in one fluid motion as the blade continues around your left side to the next movement.

9. Deliver the sweeping strike.	10. Wind up the right-side sweep.
Bring the blade around the left side and strike upward out of the rotation. Shift your weight to your front foot but don't bend your knee. Keep your back and your leg straight and taught, but not locked. The back foot should be sliding forward as you strike.	Bring the blade up on your right side, but don't bring your arms up too high. Keep them tight and close to your body to save energy and prevent yourself from being thrown off balance. Shift your weight to your back foot and step forward with the front.

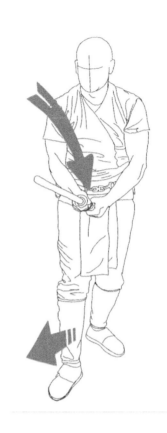

11. Deliver the right-side sweeping strike.	12. Reset to Ready Stance.
Continue to rotate the blade around the right side and shift your weight to your front foot again. Your back foot should be sliding forward as you deliver the strike, keep your back straight and don't lean into the strike too much.	Bring the saber back to your mid-line and point the blade at your enemy's throat. At the same time, shift your weight back to the back foot and slide the front foot forward.

When you complete this progression, you can repeat the movements forward infinitely as you practice maintaining form and balance. You'll also be gaining strength and training your muscle memory for the practical use of these strikes if you needed to perform one in a duel. An alternate movement for this sequence is to perform each strike while stepping backwards. The main difference here is that instead of leading with the front foot, you'll lead with the back foot each time you perform each strike.

Feel free to vary the sequence of strikes after you get good at this string of movements. You don't want your strikes to become predictable and you never know which strike you'll need to call upon at any given moment in a real duel.

Two-person Striking Practice Drill

The practice striking drill in the following section is deceptively difficult to master smoothly, while being simple enough that most anyone can understand the basic mechanics of the striking and footwork that are involved. Practice the strikes and footwork by themselves and then combine them with a partner who is also familiar with the steps.

A

Both fighters should be in the same wide stance with their right sides toward each other. Begin with hilts raised above your heads and blades pointed at the opponent's chest. The top third of your blades must be touching near the tip. The top hand guides the blade, and the bottom hand adds power to your swings. Spread your feet wide apart and keep your back straight. One fighter advances and one retreats.

B	C

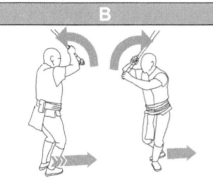 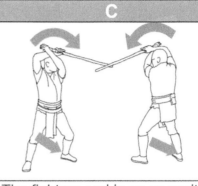

Blades raise up as they begin their rotation back for the next clash of sabers. The advancing fighter should be using the sliding step to move toward their opponent by sliding the left foot around and forward. The right foot will rotate in place when the left passes it. The retreating fighter should be using the sliding step to move backwards by sliding the right foot around and back. The left foot will rotate in place when the right passes it.	The fighters end in an opposite wide stance. The hilts are held high and the blade tips are touching and pointed at their opponent's chest. Each fighter's wrists cross over each other. The progression will repeat itself 4 times and then reverse direction with the retreating fighter now advancing and the advancing fighter now retreating.

D

Again, fighters start with sides toward each other. Hilts at chin level and blades pointed at their opponent's waist. The top third of your blades touching near the tip. The top hand guides the blade, and the bottom hand adds power to your swings. Spread your feet wide apart and keep your back straight. The same fighter to advances and one retreats.

E | F

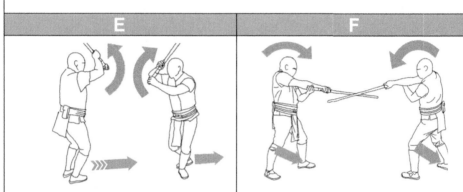

E	F
Blades raise up and begin their rotation back. The advancing fighter should be using the sliding step to move toward their opponent by sliding the left foot around and forward. The right foot will rotate in place when the left passes it. The retreating fighter should be using the sliding step to move backwards by sliding the right foot around and back. The left foot will rotate in place when the right passes it.	The fighters should end in an opposite wide stance. Blade tips are touching and pointed at the opponent's chest. The striking action has caused your wrists to cross over each other. When the blades touch this second time, you can begin your rotation the other direction. Repeat 4 times and then reverse direction with the retreating fighter now advancing and the advancing fighter now retreating.

Both fighters should be in basically the same wide stance with their right sides toward each other. Begin with hilts at eye level and blades pointed at the opponent's face. The top hand guides the blade, and the bottom hand adds power to your swings. Spread your feet wide apart and keep your back straight. Choose one fighter to advance and one to retreat.

H	I

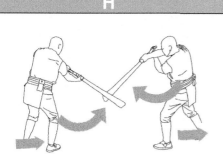

Blades sweep down toward their opponent and this time they will clash in the middle this time. The advancing fighter should be using the sliding step to move toward their opponent by sliding the left foot around and forward. The right foot will rotate in place when the left passes it. The retreating fighter should be using the sliding step to move backwards by sliding the right foot around and back. The left foot will rotate in place when the right passes it.	The fighters should end in an opposite wide stance. The hilts are still held at eye level and the tips are pointed at the opponent's face. Return the hilt to chin level on your opposite side with the tip pointing at your opponent's face. The progression will repeat itself 4 times and then reverse direction with the retreating fighter now advancing and the advancing fighter now retreating.

End of Striking Drill

With patience and practice, the moves described above can be completed in one long string of movements, Upper strikes forward (4X), Upper strikes backward (4X), then transition to Middle strikes forward (4X), Middle strikes backward (4X), Lower sweeps forward (4X), Lower sweeps backward (4X) on an infinite repeat. The more you practice this, the better and faster you will get!

Other Applications:

Apply the basic techniques to the staff!

Many duelists are attracted to exotic weapons like the double-bladed staff (because a glowing sword isn't exotic enough, apparently). Saber-staffs can be quite complicated to use effectively without striking yourself in the process. However, most of the single-bladed Form 1 strikes can be adapted for the saber-staff as well. Practice with these basic strikes can help fighters become acclimated to the staff and help them build the confidence needed to start learning the more complicated techniques.

Basic staff-wielding concepts:

Never forget that the staff has two blades. If you do, the second blade will remind you that it's the— the hard way!

Moving the staff is slower than it looks in the movies. Give yourself time to develop the strength and coordination it requires. Practice every day if you want to become more proficient.

Make sure you use the second blade to your advantage. Two-handed strikes can work with a one or two bladed saber, but the two-bladed saber has a built-in second-strike option!

Stay loose and be mindful of your grip and posture. The staff is twice as heavy as a single-bladed saber so you may lose form without realizing it. Stay in control of the staff.

Be careful not to swing too hard at your opponents. The added weight of the staff means greater momentum and it can be easy to injure an opponent if you are not careful.

2) Building Strength, Speed, and Awareness: One-Handed Techniques

It's important to work your way through the two-handed strikes and blocks, preferably against an opponent or sparring partner, before beginning this one-handed practicum. The styles are very different, but there are some important developments that happen while learning the two-handed techniques:

1) You build your strength, stamina, and blade-handling skills. All of these things will be needed with single-handed dueling. You learn how hard to hit (or how hard NOT to hit) in order to avoid causing real injuries to your opponent.

2) One important aspect of blade-handling is knowing where your body is in relation to your saber; you don't want to strike your own self during a duel! You learn the optimal distance for striking your opponent. It's important to be aware of an enemy who has entered your killzone, but it is equally important to know when you have entered their kill zone as well.

3) You learn to maintain your posture. Posture is important with any style, so developing the muscle memory to keep in correct posture is going to be an advantage for you in combat.

4) You train yourself to use the correct footwork. Footwork is incredibly important while dueling to help a fighter avoid strikes or close distance, maneuver for advantage or adjust to maintain balance while striking. Don't neglect your footwork or you will pay the price on the battlefield.

Basic Hand Positioning for 1-Handed Dueling

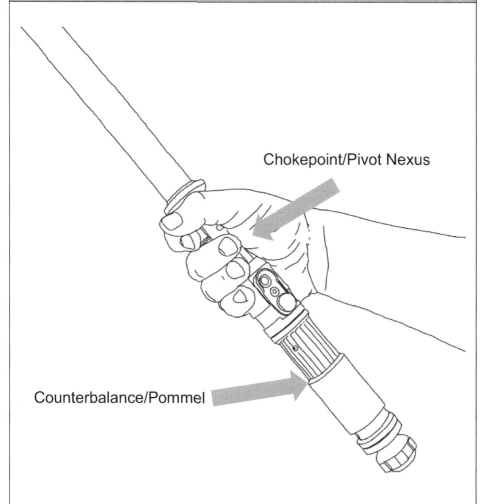

Chokepoint/Pivot Nexus

Counterbalance/Pommel

The saber should be held close to the emitter in most cases. The second finger and thumb should wrap around the upper choke-point or pivot nexus if there is one. This way the bottom portion of the hilt acts as a counterbalance for the weight of the blade.

The first, third, and fourth fingers will aid in the movement of the blade and help snap the blade into a strike.One-handed fighters will need strong, but mobile support of their sabers throughout a duel.

Basic Forward Ready Stance

Keep your feet spread apart a little wider than shoulder width apart. Be careful not to spread your feet too far apart or you will end up throwing yourself off balance. Spread your weight evenly between your feet. Aim your saber at your opponent's throat and keep your grip should be firm, yet fluid. Your off-hand can be placed in a fist at your chest or by your side. As you duel you will need to use this hand to help balance, but when it is not being used, you should keep it inside your body line to prevent it from becoming a target. There are other positions for the off-hand (behind the back, steadying the sword-hand, etc.) but the basic concept is the same: keep the hand out of the way until you need it! Your back should be strong, yet supple—be ready to move at a moment's notice. I tend to lean forward over my forward knee a little bit to protect that limb and prevent my opponent from using it as a target.

Wide Switch-Stance

The footing for this stance is opposite of the Basic Forward Stance. The blade remains in the same hand but it is brought up alongside the fighter's face. The middle and pointer fingers of the off-hand are pointed at your opponent (also called "sword-fingers"). The tip of the blade is pointed either at your opponent's throat or their chest. The feet are spread wide; allow yourself to sink into a deeper "riding-stance" than you did with the Forward Stance. And keep your thighs tight. Your back should be straight and tight. This stance is a minor taunt to your opponent who may think they have an easy shot at your legs or your outstretched arm. WATCH their movements and strike when the time is right!!

Low (Reverse) Guard

Everything about this stance is about potential energy. You are wound up and ready to strike! Weight is on the front foot and your body is leaning toward your opponent. The saber is held behind you and the tip is pointed at the floor. Resist the urge to rest the tip of the saber on the ground. The tip should be held just above the ground. The off-hand should be held in front of your face in a focusing maneuver as you ready yourself to strike your opponent.

Low (forward) Guard

The basic position of this guard is essentially the same as the Basic Forward Stance, but the blade tip has been lowered and is pointed at the floor. The shoulders should appear relaxed but remain mobile and loose. Your off-hand can rest at your side or even be held behind your back. This guard position is a taunt at your opponent and is intended to make the opponent believe that your guard has dropped and you are unprepared to attack or defend yourself. This is not true, of course as speed is the essence of one-handed dueling, and you are capable of bringing your saber up quickly to fend off your enemy's strikes or deliver a cutting blow to them if they enter your circle.

Principles of Bladework

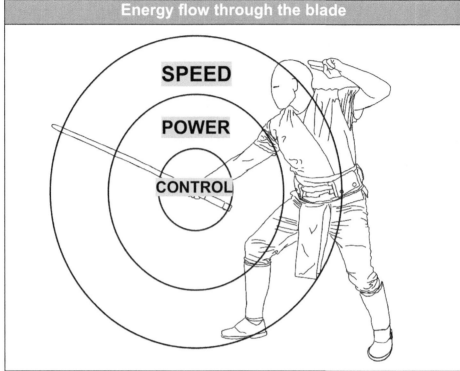

Energy flow through the blade

SPEED

POWER

CONTROL

Single-handed fighters use slightly different fighting principles than a two-handed fighter.

- The top half of the blade is ideal for **speed**. Use quick strikes and last second deflections while keeping your opponent at a distance.
- The bottom half of the blade delivers more **power** in your strikes, but relies on bringing you in closer to your enemy.
- The **control** of the hilt still comes from the hand, but this time, the striking motion does not have the benefit of the second hand for the "push and pull" motion described in the previous two-handed section of the book. Be aware of your hilt, and be sure not to allow your opponent's blade to bounce off of your blade and strike you unintentionally.

There are many different variations of the basic strike in the one-handed style. Some examples of different strikes are demonstrated on the following pages, all originating from the basic one-handed forward ready stance which is explained on the next page.

Basic Forward Ready Stance

Keep your feet spread a little wider than shoulder width but be careful not to spread your feet too far apart or you will end up throwing yourself off balance or have difficulty moving fluidly. Distribute your weight evenly between your feet. Your front foot should be pointing at your opponent and your back foot should be at a 45-degree angle. Don't plant your foot, but keep it mobile. Your saber should be aimed at your opponent's throat and your grip should be firm, yet fluid. Your off-hand can be placed in a fist at your chest. As you duel you will need to use this hand to help balance yourself, but when it is not being used, you should keep it inside your body line to prevent it from becoming a target. There are other positions for the off-hand, but the basic concept is the same; keep the hand out of the way until you need it! Your back should be strong, yet supple—Don't let yourself be a sitting target! Move yourself around the combat area constantly and keep searching for an advantage over your opponent. Keep your blade moving as well, so your opponent doesn't know when you're going to strike!

In this style, the blade is lead by the hilt through its range of motion by pushing the hilt forward and snapping the blade into its target at the precise moment (see the following pages).

1. Ready position	2. Lead the strike	3. Snap the blade

Begin in Forward Ready position, keep the legs loose and mobile, held wide apart. Bend your knees slightly and spread your weight evenly between your feet. Don't lean forward. (see the previous page for more details.)	Lead hilt in front of your body. Keep your 2nd finger and thumb tight around the hilt and loosen the 3rd and 4th fingers while slightly tightening the 1st finger. Allow the blade-tip to stay in place as the saber hilt moves forward and winds up the strike.	Once the blade is wound up, you can use the forward motion of your arm to to snap the tip of the blade forward with your wrist and fingers. The 2nd finger is the pivot and the 3rd and 4th fingers now tighten on the hilt to snap the blade forward against the palm of the hand and the fingers tighten their grip. Once the strike is delivered, prepare your next move.

Strike sequence 1: Right Sweeping Strike

Begin in the Forward Ready Stance. Your eyes should be on the face of your enemy and your peripheral vision should be watching for movement.	Begin the strike by winding the blade backwards around the shoulder. Use the weight of the blade to help propel the blade around.	Continue the rotation of the blade around your side. The off-hand can begin to help you find your balance as you rotate the blade around.	Guide the hilt with your loose fingers and prepare to snap the hilt against your palm in the next action.	Use your arm to extend the blade forward as you use your loose fingers to snap the blade quickly against your palm.

Strike sequence 2: Backhand Strike

Use your arm to extend the blade forward as you use your loose fingers to snap the blade quickly against your palm	Guide the hilt with your loose fingers and prepare to snap the hilt against your palm in the next action.	Continue the rotation of the blade across your front. Keep the off-hand out of the way as you rotate the blade around.	Begin the strike by winding the blade in front of you. Use the weight of the blade to help propel the blade around.	Begin in the Forward Ready Stance. Your eyes should be on the face of your enemy and your peripheral vision should be watching for movement.

Striking with Footwork

Footwork while striking one-handed involves roughly the same principles as the two-handed style. The fighter should step (either an advancing or retreating step) as the strike winds up, and then bring the other foot in to return the fighter to the ready position for the next action (strike, block, parry, or evade). However, duels are very chaotic by nature and strikes can occur as an opening presents itself, but these are general guidelines for fighters to help them maintain their balance in a duel. An off-balance fighter becomes the victim of someone else's designs.

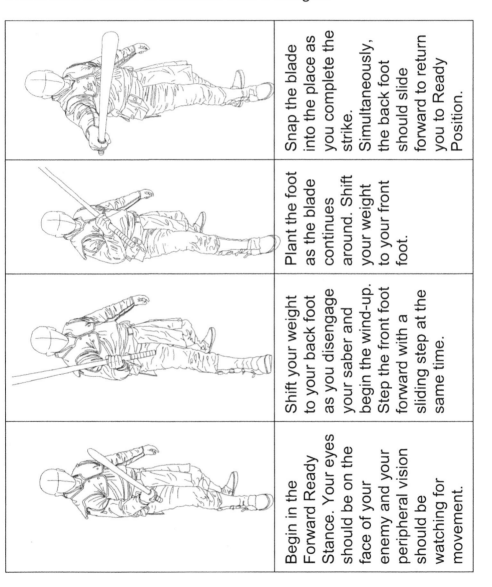

(top)	Snap the blade into the place as you complete the strike. Simultaneously, the back foot should slide forward to return you to Ready Position.
	Plant the foot as the blade continues around. Shift your weight to your front foot.
	Shift your weight to your back foot as you disengage your saber and begin the wind-up. Step the front foot forward with a sliding step at the same time.
(bottom)	Begin in the Forward Ready Stance. Your eyes should be on the face of your enemy and your peripheral vision should be watching for movement.

Blocking Movemements

Each of the blocking movements begin from the Forward Ready Stance. As you perform a blocking movement, try to get into the habit of stepping backwards with at least your back foot to put more distance between you and your opponent.

Right Forward Block	Left Forward Block

From a basic Ready stance, disengage and swivel your saber arm at your elbow to either side, depending on the side that you are trying to block. Notice how the front foot slides backwards for the Left Forwad Block to prevent it from becoming a target during battle.

Right Backhanded Block	Left Backhanded Block

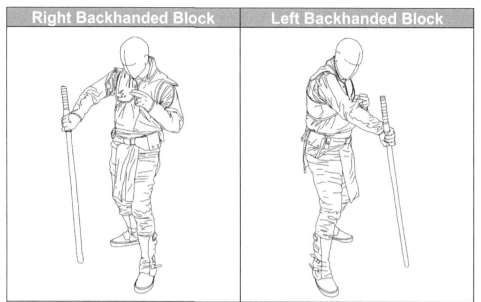

These blocks provide an excellent opportunity to transition into a parry against your opponent. For the Left side, Drop the blade of the saber down in a sweeping motion. Stop there for a simple block or continue around for a parry by clearing your opponent's blade and leaving them open.

Right Lower Block	Left Lower Block

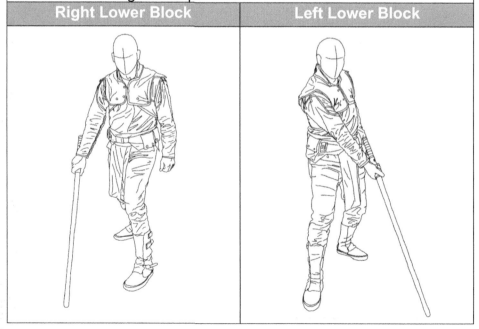

Right Upper Block	Left Upper Block

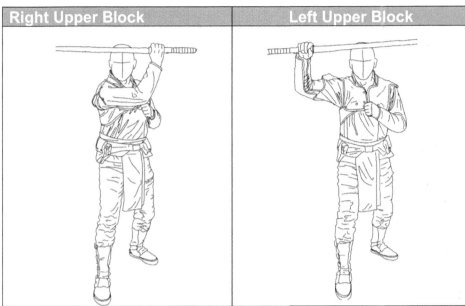

These blocks are less mobile than the previous set, but they still provide opportunities to control your opponent's blade by sweeping your saber out and deflecting their strike. As you raise your blade up for the block/parry, you also extend it out away from your body so your blade doesn't get knocked into you.

Right Reverse Block	Left Reverse Block

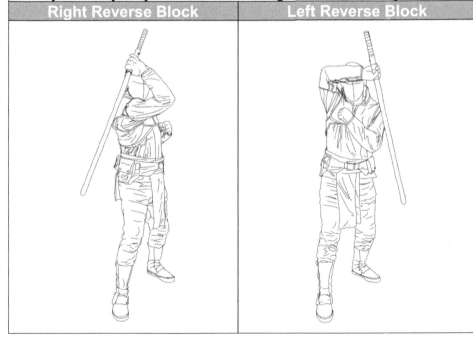

The Senseless Spin (one-handed continuous orbit)

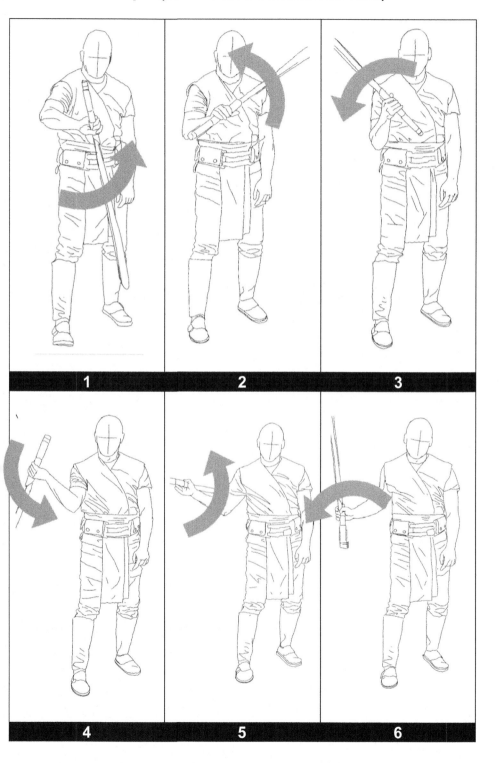

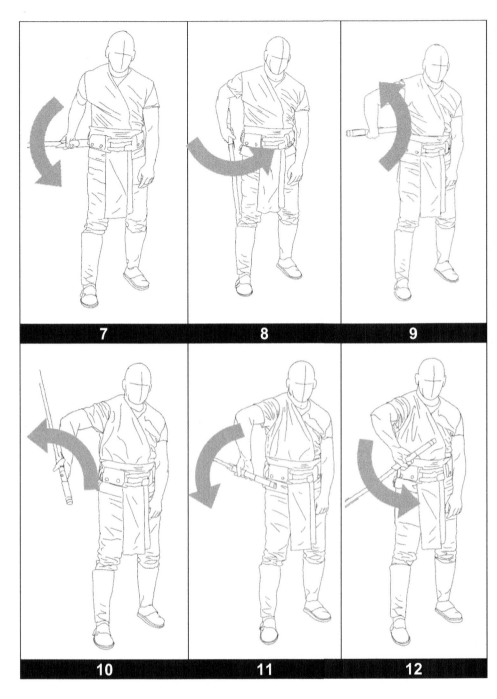

Let the weight of your blade carry the rotation through. Once you reach step 12, repeat all steps continuously. Keep your legs out of the way as you spin and keep at it until the spin is fluid.

Each style and stance has its own applications and benefits. When practicing, visualize your weak spots and try to predict where an enemy will strike so you can be ready. Your opponent will look for opportunities to evade your strikes or attack an opening. Be sure that you are ready.

Know yourself, and you will begin to know your adversaries.

4)　　The Art of the Duel:
Technique in Action
(or *How to Seriously Pretend*)

When dueling an opponent, never assume that your intended strike will automatically land where you are aiming. You must assume that they have also trained and practiced with a laser sword and are able to handle their saber. It's always wise to have a second action ready to go after you launch your first strike so you can either strike a second location after they have moved their blade to block yours, or so you can block their incoming attempt to strike you after your unsuccessful attempt.

The lightsaber is meant to be a 360° blade that is made from a continuously circulating arc of energy that will cut through almost anything. It's not necessary to exert an extreme amount of power through your strikes. In other words, you don't need to hit hard to get a successful strike! A simple tap from a blade of this sort will be enough to maim or even kill an opponent if these were real arc-wave blades.

Some of my dueling group's liveliest debates have been around the topic of how hard to hit your opponent. When we first started teaching ourselves this sport, we would be covered with welts and bruises after each session. After a while, we began to realize one important fact about our technique: the guys who hit the hardest were not the most successful.

In my experience, fighters who really used their strength to push their strikes were actually slowing themselves down because they were too tense! Fighters who favored more fluid strikes, and who made smaller and more direct movements during their strikes, were more successful. One reason for this is because of a principle called:

Economy of Movement.

Put simply, "Economy of Movement," means that you would have less "wind-up" to your strikes and thus, more immediate action. Harder strikes are slower than many softer strikes because they require much more energy to put into action. You have to pull the blade back farther before you strike. Your body will be tense and rigid, which will slow you down. Your accuracy will be worse because your energy is devoted more to the power in the swing than to the position of the blade. It's wise training to strike quickly, but...

-speed is not the same as power-

When a fighter sees an opening, they should move the blade to make contact with their opponent in the shortest route possible. As a result, you may end up hitting softer, but you will have quicker strikes with greater accuracy than if you were attempting to swing the blade with so much force that you split the fabric of reality (or actually injure your opponent) in the process.

As a serious duelist, it's important to consider the health and well-being of your opponent and make sure that you are striking quickly, but not with enough force or in such a way as to actually cause harm to them, or yourself. I have had black eyes, split lips, bruises, welts, broken glasses, and many smacks to the head that helped to teach me this lesson so that I may pass this information along to you.

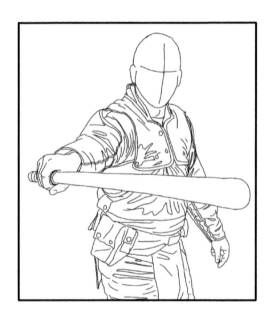

The "Circle of Death"

Whether you are dueling two-handed or one-handed, you can think of the area around you as your space to control in a duel. Anything within reach of your saber in a 360° field around your center mass is subject to your will. This is your Circle of Death. If your opponent or their blade enters your circle, then it's your duty as a swordsman to handle the intruder however you see fit. Remember that YOU must control your space— if you don't, your opponent will and the confrontation will end in your defeat.

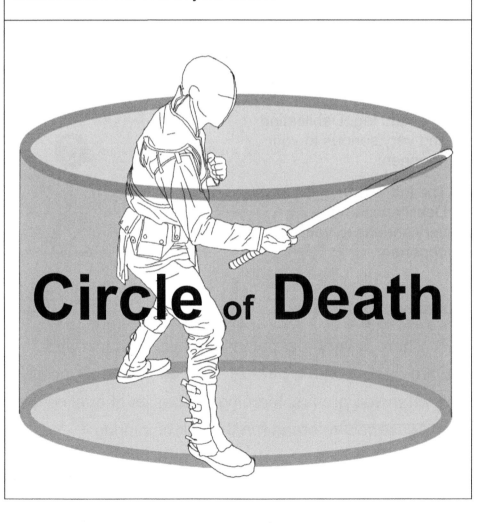

Strike Zones

There are six generally accepted regions where you can strike your opponent. These regions are called Strike Zones and consist of:

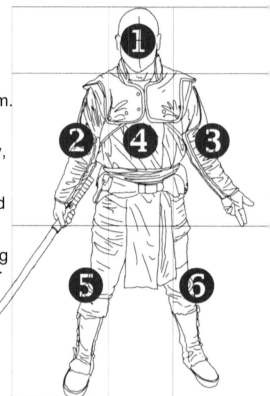

1. The head. A strike here would be an instant kill.

2. The right arm. This is typically the weapon-arm.

3. The left arm. The off-hand; a painful injury, but not fatal.

4. The torso. A serious and
5. most likely fatal wound.

6. The right leg. Debilitating and very serious to your opponent.

7. The left leg.
8. Debilitating and very serious to your opponent.

Protective Equipment

There is very real potential for bodily harm when you are dueling with a partner. That danger is especially high when you are first learning the basics of dueling, but even seasoned veterans run the risk of injuring themselves or someone else during the chaos of battle.

Wearing protective equipment is not only good dueling practice, it's also required by many saber-fighting organizations around the globe.

When searching for a saber-fighting organization to join, or if you are starting your own club, give serious thought to the amount and type of protection that you and your opponents will be wearing. A fat lip and/or a black eye can be a hard lesson that you could avoid if you start thinking about this now!

There are several different types of armor that are available, but if you choose to, you can make your own! The equipment shown here was created by me to be worn as my dueling persona Captain Maberu. Most of this dueling kit was based on ancient Japanese Samurai and Ninja armor. Pieces included:

American Fencing Helmet

3-layer Manchira jacket (modified)

Kimono (Shitagi)

White stretchy denim jeans

T-shirt

Athletic cup (not shown)

Broomball gloves

Vinyl Gaiters

Comfortable shoes

Below are three items that are *must-haves* for dueling to protect your vital areas.

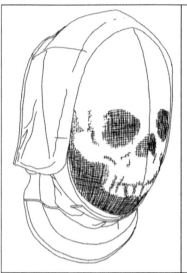	A fencing-type helmet is crucial to protect your face. The helmet shown here is mine, with custom paint for intimidation purposes. When worn correctly these helmets can offer excellent protection against head-shots and have good breathability during a duel. They are also relatively lightweight (once you get used to it) and allow you to have adequate visibility. It also has the added function of deadening the noise from a head-shot.
	Even if the hands are not a valid strike zone, accidental hand strikes do happen and they are extremely painful if you aren't wearing gloves. Lacrosse, broomball, and hockey gloves have the best padding and protect the hands well while still providing flexibility. Some saber organizations are marketing their own gloved to fighter and they are worth taking a look at.
	The final piece of equipment on this list is the Athletic cup. These are overlooked by many fighters and have a wide range in price. Just get the cheapest one in your size and that should be fine.

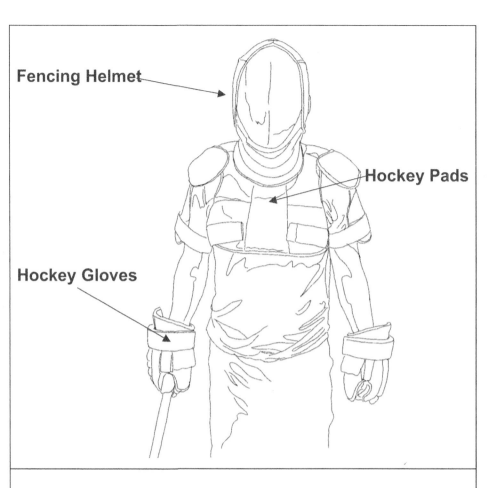

Fencing Helmet

Hockey Pads

Hockey Gloves

An additional piece of equipment that can offer some extra protection and peace-of-mind in a duel is some sort of body-protection for your upper torso. Hockey, Baseball, and Lacrosse pads do an excellent job of protecting the top half of your body. You can also use motorcycle pads, body armor, or anything else that would give you protection from injury—just be sure that you still have adequate protection so you can avoid getting hurt! Remember: many dueling organizations REQUIRE you to wear protective pads as a condition of your participation! No pads, no duel! Baseball protection, Hockey gloves, Standard fencing helmet are shown above.

In a real-time duel, fighters have to make split-second decisions to stay alive; they may deliver a strike, parry, or block to their opponent depending on the circumstances. Many beginning duelists have the habit of "sleeping on their strikes" when they first begin to strike out at their adversaries in the combat arena. In other words, they deliver a strike, and then hang there in the strike position for a beat or two and leave themselves wide open to retaliation from their opponent. They may be thinking about their next action, or trying to mentally register whether they have made a valid strike, but they are missing one very important point.

Newton's third law states that for every action there is an equal or opposite reaction (for example, you strike at your opponent, and they deflect it), but not every strike is successful. Strikes may be blocked, deflected, or simply avoided by your opponent, so you need to have a second action ready after you strike, or after you complete any action, really. Many fighters don't plan to hit with their first strike and use it

as a lure to create an opening in their opponent's form or expose a weakness. Once they have done that, then they go for the killing stroke.

It's important to train yourself to strike quickly and accurately, but it is equally important to train yourself to snap into the next action before your opponent gets the chance to take advantage of your open strike points. Remember that dueling is not one-sided; your opponent is trying to score against you as you try to score against them. Be prepared for them to be looking for their second action as well.

If you just sit in one spot while you fight, your opponent can, will, and should begin circling you to try and suss out a weak spot or potential chance to strike. A good fighter can also use movement to maneuver their opponent into a trap, or a position that's going to land them in danger. You can avoid that by countering their movements and even begin to put the pressure back on them by moving around. However, according to the principle of economy of movement, you don't want to move too much! If you're running around doing flips or bouncing off of the walls, you will undoubtedly tire yourself out, leave yourself wide open, and end up getting killed. Slight movements are all you need.

Also, if you stay in one spot for too long you will tend to start settling in and planting your feet, which will slow you down and make you a sitting duck! Don't let that happen to you!

Remember to **D. R. I. L. L.**

> ➢ **D**o it.
> ➢ **R**e-do it.
> ➢ **I**mitate what you just did.
> ➢ **L**earn to keep doing it.
> ➢ **L**ive the rest of your life doing it.

There are many fighters and experts out there who say that there's no place for fancy techniques in "real" dueling, but if that's what you want to do, don't let anyone stop you! The trick is to practice that specific skill over and over and figure out what works and what doesn't. Then put it into action. Make it work for you, but know your limitations and abilities, and always, always, ALWAYS consider the safety of your opponent. If what you are trying to do is going to hurt you or your opponent, stop immediately! Rethink what you are doing and figure out how to make it work s-a-f-e-l-y.

Of course, many of the techniques that are used in the movies are not physically possible in this galaxy. There are groups who practice choreographed routines which include force pushes and acrobatic maneuvers, which are not covered in this volume. This book is focused on unchoreographed, real-time swordplay.

Keep in mind that the goal of the duel is for one of the fighters to be able to walk away. Suicide strikes and hail-Mary lunges may get you a point, but many groups have rules against that type of fighting and can even penalize a fighter by giving the point to your opponent! You will likely get hit after you have completed a strike; that happens frequently. Just don't plan for it to happen that way—that's sloppy dueling with a weapon that is intended to be elegant and civilized.

New duelists often have a hard time as they begin the sport because they lose their first duels. Sometimes they lose A LOT. Some even give up before they discover their true potential. What they fail to realize is that, with training and practice new students can quickly improve their skills and begin to be truly competitive in a duel.

"Guard that leg!!!"

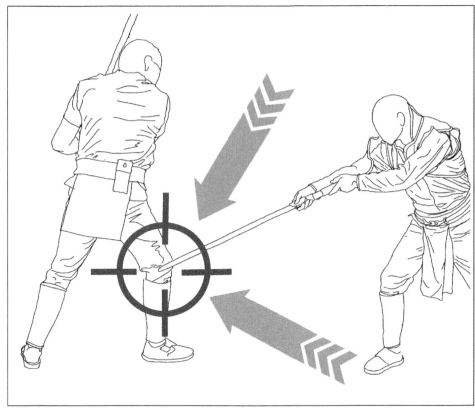

Often in the frenzy of a battle, beginning fighters tend to think that the entire fight is in the blade of their weapon. It's easy to forget about our other body parts when we're in the middle of a heated duel against an opponent and leave an arm or a leg out in the open to become a target. It only takes one quick swipe to make a successful attack against an unguarded limb and then retreat unharmed. Don't let this happen to you!

Alternatively, as a fighter you should always be aware of opportunities like an open limb or an unprotected side. Don't be afraid to take advantage of any opportunity to overcome your enemy. Feel your opponent out as you duel and see where they have openings or weaknesses in their form—then strike!

When you get to be more aware and able to attack and defend more efficiently, you can start to play around with the fighting forms and maybe pretend to leave a leg out in the open to entice your opponent. If you can lure them closer to your Circle of Death you can lure them closer to their demise.

Always be aware of your body. Your gaze should be focused on your opponent and your peripheral vision should be active and constantly aware of yourself, your opponent, and your environment! It takes time and practice to increase your awareness.

There are dozens of scenes in the movies of two master Jedi knights locking their blades together in intense fury until the action explodes from in between their fiery clash! These scenes are so popular that many lightsabers even have special buttons for sound and light effects that allow you to successfully mimic that scene with your friends.

However, in a real duel these types of lock-ups are not very practical and are very easy to get out of and leave your opponent open to a quick strike to the head, or a simple tap after a push-off disengagement from one of the fighters. Don't attempt to do this in an actual duel or you will get killed. Fast.

It's important to train in different styles and techniques so you have more things in your "toolbox" in a duel if you need to try and switch things up. The last thing that you want is to become predictable! A smart adversary will pick up on that quickly and take you out!

Important attributes for a swordfighter to have:

- ❖ **Physical conditioning-** Modern people are nowhere near as tough as our ancestors; especially in our core. Cardio and strong wrists are important for sword fighting.
- ❖ **Mental aspects-** situational awareness, calmness under pressure, serenity, self-confidence, and toughness of spirit.
- ❖ **Deception-** Foul play is often expected in a true duel to the death, but real-time duelists won't want to duel the "guy with all of the dirty tricks." Just remember that fake-outs and misdirection rely on your opponent's judgement (or lack of) to work—if a fighter falls for your ruse, that's their own fault! They'll probably be ready for it the next time you try and use it though!
- ❖ **Rhythm-** Each duel will have its own beat and its own score, but predictability will get you killed.

Don't fall into a pattern or your opponent will take advantage of it.

❖ **Intimidation-** If you get inside your opponent's head the duel is yours. Just remember that this is supposed to be fun for everyone involved so don't get personal!

❖ **Timing-** Figuring out when to strike and how close to be to your opponent when an opportunity presents itself are important, yet difficult skills to master. Through practice and training you could learn to use the timing of a duel to your advantage.

❖ **Spatial Awareness-** There are times when it seems super easy to get the first strike against your opponent, but the second strike always seems to fall on you. A good fighter focuses their awareness on their opponent, themselves, and their surroundings.

❖ **Caution-** To be clear, this is not the same as timidity. This is about having enough sense that you don't underestimate your opponents or take unnecessary risks.

A wise and skillful duelist once said, "Your focus determines your reality." That's as true with dueling as it is with any skill. If you focus on your training and are committed to improving your skills, you will see improvement in your style every time.

Deciding what to do next…

There are several different options for expressing your love of lightsaber dueling. I'm going to assume that most fighters would want to go on to fight more opponents than your same group of 3 or 4 friends every time. To do that you'll need to start getting some new members. There are several options:

❖ **Join an existing group in your area.**

Most of the larger metropolitan areas appear to have at least one lightsaber dueling group actively dueling in parks, parking garages, or fields around the city. Start doing your research; Google is a logical first step. Make sure that you visit local collectible shows, Star Wars premiers, and other geeky places where you might be able to get information about the group. Then make contact! Different groups have different requirements for participation and may require you to have protective gear before you are allowed to participate, so be sure to ask what their requirements are before you sign up!

❖ **Represent one of the larger national groups with your own local charter.**

If you start along the Lightsaber dueling path via internet searches and research, you will find that the larger groups often have certain requirements listed on their webpages for membership or creation of your own charter of their specific organization. If you find a group whose fighting style you like, then there is no need to reinvent the wheel. Simply go through the steps to create your own branch and you'll be on your way! Just be sure that you adhere to that group's rules and requirements to maintain your charter and keep a healthy relationship with your main group.

❖ **Create your own fighting and rule system in your area.**

My group, the Central Republic began as a way to fill the vacuum that existed in our area for lightsaber dueling groups. A small group of us felt driven to improve our skills with the lightsaber and share our love for the sport with each other. When there was no group in our area, we did copious amounts of research and tried to figure out what we wanted our group to look like. We cherry-picked things that we liked from other groups and melded what we were already doing in our meetings with what we wanted to be, and that became the Central Republic.

The following rules are specific to The Central Republic and are reviewed with new members.

Duels can be very fast-paced and chaotic so we rely on the honor system for calling strikes. Fighters who are not dueling may act as referees if requested. "Trades" or simultaneous strikes do not count as a point for either fighter and the duel resets. If a fighter touches themselves with any part of the blade while dueling, it counts as a strike for their opponent and combat will be reset.

The valid strike zones are: the head (with approved helmet and facemask only), above the elbow to the shoulder, above the knee to the hip, and the front and back of the torso (The basic Darth Vader). The face and groin are not targets, and should be avoided as much as possible. Accidental saber contact with the groin area will result in a point for the wounded fighter and 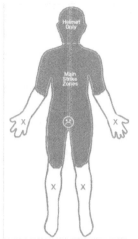 pause the match until such time as the fighter recovers. Intentional strikes to your opponent's face or groin are not permitted and will result in a forfeiture of match. Any strikes done in anger will cause a forfeit for the offending party.

Do not block or grab your opponent's blade with your hands, forearms, feet or legs. Doing so will award the point to your opponent and reset the match. Intentional grappling, wrestling, kicking, or making contact with your opponent using anything but the blade of your saber is not permitted.

Each fighter must be sure that they do not intentionally cause injury to their opponent. Control is the essence of the duel and each participant must be aware of their own skill level. Be respectful of your opponents and lower your skill level to meet less experienced fighters and even the playing field.

No lunging, stabbing, or strikes that cause the tip of your saber to come into contact with your opponent in a thrusting manner are permitted. Occasionally, the tip of your saber may brush your opponent in a lateral sweeping or glancing strike; that is permitted.

Protective equipment is important to help fighters avoid injury and is required for participation in TCR dueling. The bare minimum required equipment is: protective gloves, proper shoes, and a fencing-type helmet with a face-mask. Airsoft face coverings and/or face coverings with a plastic visor are not permitted. Additional protective gear (such as body armor or an athletic cup) can be worn at each fighter's discretion, but are welcome. Dueling in costume is recommended, but the costume must not restrict your movement, impede your vision or contain any items that would cause injury to an opponent.

We recommend using a dueling-specific saber because they have sturdier blades and will not break easily. Hasbro, Force FX, and Black Series sabers WILL break under the stress of a duel. Please be aware that fighters bear the responsibility of replacing or repairing their own equipment if it is damaged in a duel or practice exercise.

We must always fight with honor, in order to ensure that we always have opponents to fight with.

You can find lightsabers online simply by doing an internet search, but there are a few groups you should know (I am not endorsed by any of these groups… well, except the last one).

- **Sabersourcing:**
  They are THE source for saber knowledge if you are looking to buy a saber, check them out first. They are on YouTube.
- **Terra Prime Light Armory (TPLA):**
  TPLA is one of the best resources for lightsaber and dueling info. Find them on YouTube, they have breakdowns of all 7 official forms.
- **Saberforge:**
  They have a great selection of high-quality sabers at a decent price compared with other vendors of similar quality. In my opinion the best thing about them is their ASP saber parts that let you customize your own piece from their parts! Try their website or their Etsy store.
- **Sabertrio:**
  High quality sabers at a decent price for all of the options that you get.
- **Ultrasabers:**
  These guys often get a bad rap in the saber community, but in my opinion, they have great sabers and options at great prices. They usually ship surprisingly fast as well.
- **YDD and LGT sabers:**
  A lot of saber dealers are actually reselling these sabers at a markup. Familiarize yourself with their lines so you can know what you're looking at next time you see a "discount saber" dealer online.
- **Vader's vault:**
  They sell very high-quality sabers, but they are a bit pricey compared with the others. Is it worth it? You be the judge!
- **Starfall Sabers:**
  These are one-of-a-kind custom "bucket-list" sabers that you can find on Instagram and Etsy. Their designs will blow your mind!
- There are many Light Saber groups online:
  Lightspeed Saber League
  Ludosport
  Saber Legion
  Just to name a few…

The Central Republic (my home group):
Okay, this group I am endorsed by; this is the Saber fighting group that I belong to in Central California. You can find us on Instagram or Facebook and see what we do. @Central_Republic

THE END

NOTES:

Printed in Great Britain
by Amazon

21967649R00067